Praye

Copyright © 2011 by the compiler of this book Rdr. Symeon Campbell
All rights reserved.
ISBN: 9781467973724

Table of Contents

	Page
Morning Prayers	Page 7
Evening Prayers	Page 25
The Order of Preparation for Communion	Page 41
Canon of Preparation for Holy Communion	Page 47
A Preparation of Confession by St. John Kronstadt	Page 75
Appendix A	Page 79
Appendix B	Page 81
Prayer List for The Living	Page 85
Prayer List for The Departed	Page 91

Orthodox Daily Prayers

Morning Prayers

*[If for some legitimate reason you are not able to recite the full prayer rule, you may say the prayers in **bold type** omitting the others]*

+ In the Name of the Father, and of the Son, and of the Holy Spirit. Amen.

Prayer of the Publican
O God, be merciful to me, a sinner. *Thrice.*

Glory to Thee, our God, glory to Thee.

Between Pascha and Pentecost we omit "O Heavenly King" and say the following: **Christ is risen from the dead, trampling down death by death, and upon those in the tombs, bestowing life. Thrice.**

O Heavenly King *Tone 6*
O Heavenly King, Comforter, Spirit of Truth, Who art everywhere present and fillest all things, Treasury of good things and Giver of Life, come and dwell in us, and cleanse us of all impurity, and save our souls, O Good One.

Trisagion
Holy God, Holy Mighty, Holy Immortal, have mercy on us. *Thrice.*

Glory to the Father, and to the Son and to the Holy Spirit, both now and ever, and unto the ages of ages. Amen.

O Most Holy Trinity, have mercy on us. O Lord blot out our sins. O Master, pardon our iniquities. O Holy One, visit and heal our infirmities for Thy name's sake.

Lord Have Mercy. *Thrice.*

Glory to the Father, and to the Son and to the Holy Spirit, both now and ever, and unto the ages of ages. Amen.

Our Father, Who art in the heavens, hallowed be Thy Name. Thy Kingdom come. Thy will be done, on earth as it is in heaven. Give us this day our daily bread. And forgive us our debts as we forgive our debtors. And lead us not into temptation, but deliver us from the evil one.

Troparia to the Holy Trinity:
Having risen from sleep, we fall down before Thee, O Good One, and we cry aloud to Thee the angelic hymn, O Mighty One: Holy, Holy, Holy art Thou, O God; through the Theotokos, have mercy on us.

Glory to the Father, and to the Son, and to the Holy Spirit.

From bed and sleep hast Thou raised me up, O Lord; enlighten my mind and heart, and open my lips that I may hymn Thee, O Holy Trinity: Holy, Holy, Holy art Thou, O God; through the Theotokos, have mercy on us.

Both now and ever, and unto the ages of ages. Amen.

Suddenly the Judge shall come, and the deeds of each shall be laid bare; but with fear do we cry at midnight: Holy, Holy, Holy art Thou, O God; through the Theotokos, have mercy on us.

Lord, have mercy. *Twelve times.*

Prayer of Saint Basil the Great to the Most Holy Trinity:
As I rise from sleep, I thank Thee, O Holy Trinity, for through Thy great goodness and patience Thou hast not been angry with me, an idler and sinner, nor hast Thou destroyed me with mine iniquities, but hast shown Thy usual love for mankind; and when I was prostrate in despair, Thou hast raised me up to keep the morning watch and glorify Thy power. And now enlighten my mind's eye, and open my mouth that I may meditate on Thy words, and understand Thy commandments, and do Thy will, and hymn Thee in heartfelt confession, and sing praises to Thine all-holy name: of the Father, and of the

Son, and of the Holy Spirit, now and ever, and unto the ages of ages. Amen.

O Come, let us worship God, our King.
Bow.
O Come, let us worship and fall down before Christ, our King and God.
Bow.
O Come, let us worship and fall down before Christ himself, our King and God.
Bow.

Psalm 50

Have mercy on me, O God, according to Thy great mercy; and according to the multitude of Thy compassions blot out my transgression. Wash me thoroughly from mine iniquity, and cleanse me from my sin. For I know mine iniquity, and my sin is ever before me. Against Thee only have I sinned and done this evil before Thee, that Thou mightest be justified in Thy words, and prevail when Thou art judged. For behold, I was conceived in iniquities, and in sins did my mother bear me. For behold, Thou hast loved truth; the hidden and secret things of Thy wisdom hast Thou made manifest unto me. Thou shalt sprinkle me with hyssop, and I shall be made clean; Thou shalt wash me, and I shall be made whiter than snow. Thou shalt make me to hear joy and gladness; the bones that be humbled, they shall rejoice. Turn Thy face away from my sins, and blot out all mine iniquities. Create in me a clean heart, O God, and renew a right spirit within me. Cast me not away from Thy presence, and take not Thy Holy Spirit from me. Restore unto me the joy of Thy salvation and with Thy governing Spirit establish me. I shall teach transgressors Thy ways, and the ungodly shall turn back unto Thee. Deliver me from blood-guiltiness, O God, Thou God of my salvation; my tongue shall rejoice in Thy righteousness. O Lord, Thou shalt open my lips, and my mouth shall declare Thy praise. For if Thou hadst desired sacrifice, I had given it; with whole-burnt offerings Thou shalt not be pleased. A sacrifice unto God is a broken spirit; a heart that is broken and humbled God will not despise. Do good, O Lord, in Thy good pleasure unto Sion, and let the walls of Jerusalem be builded. Then shalt Thou be pleased with a sacrifice of righteousness, with oblation and whole-burnt offerings. Then shall they offer bullocks upon Thine altar.

The Symbol of the Orthodox Faith
I believe in one God, the Father Almighty, Maker of Heaven and earth, and of all things visible and invisible. And in one Lord Jesus Christ, the Son of God, the Only-begotten, begotten of the Father before all ages; Light of Light: true God of true God; begotten, not made; of one essence with the Father, by Whom all things were made; Who for us men, and for our salvation, came down from the heavens, and was incarnate of the Holy

Spirit and the Virgin Mary, and became man; And was crucified for us under Pontius Pilate, and suffered, and was buried; And arose again on the third day according to the Scriptures; And ascended into the heavens, and sitteth at the right hand of the Father; And shall come again, with glory, to judge both the living and the dead; Whose kingdom shall have no end. And in the Holy Spirit, the Lord, the Giver of Life; Who proceedeth from the Father; Who with the Father and the Son together is worshipped and glorified; Who spake by the prophets. In One, Holy, Catholic, and Apostolic Church. I confess one baptism for the remission of sins. I look for the resurrection of the dead, And the life of the age to come. Amen.

Prayer 1, of St. Macarius the Great
O God, cleanse me, a sinner, for I have never done anything good in Thy sight; but deliver me from the evil one, and let Thy will be in me, that I may open mine unworthy mouth without condemnation, and praise Thy holy Name of the Father, and the Son and the Holy Spirit, now and ever, and unto the ages of ages. Amen.

Prayer 2, of the same saint
Having risen from sleep, I offer unto Thee, O Saviour, the midnight hymn, and falling down I cry unto thee: Grant me not to fall asleep in the death of sin, but have compassion on me, O Thou Who wast voluntarily crucified, and hasten to raise me

who am reclining in idleness, and save me in prayer and intercession; and after the night's sleep shine upon me a sinless day, O Christ God, and save me.

Prayer 3, of the same saint
Having risen from sleep, I hasten to Thee, O Master, Lover of mankind, and by Thy loving-kindness, I strive to do Thy work, and I pray to Thee: Help me at all times, in everything, and deliver me from every worldly, evil thing and every impulse of the devil, and save me and lead me into Thine eternal kingdom. For Thou art my Creator, and the Giver and Provider of everything good, and in Thee is all my hope, and unto Thee do I send up glory, now and ever, and unto the ages of ages. Amen.

Prayer 4, of the same saint
O Lord, Who in Thine abundant goodness and Thy great compassion hast granted me, Thy servant, to go through the time of the night that is past without attack from any opposing evil: Do Thou Thyself, O Master and Creator of all things, vouchsafe me by Thy true light and with an enlightened heart to do Thy will, now and ever, and unto the ages of ages. Amen.

Prayer 5, of St. Basil the Great
O Lord Almighty, God of hosts and of all flesh, Who dwellest on high and lookest down on things that are lowly, Who searchest our hearts and innermost being, and clearly foreknowest the secrets of men; O unoriginate and everlasting Light, in Whom is no variableness, neither shadow of turning; Do Thou, O

Immortal King, receive our supplications which we, daring because of the multitude of Thy compassions, offer Thee at the present time from defiled lips; and forgive us our sins, in deed, word, and thought, whether committed by us knowingly or in ignorance, and cleanse us from every defilement of flesh and spirit. And grant us to pass through the night of the whole present life with watchful heart and sober thought, ever expecting the coming of the bright and appointed day of Thine Only-begotten Son, our Lord and God and Saviour, Jesus Christ, whereon the Judge of all shall come with glory to reward each according to his deeds. May we not be found fallen and idle, but watching, and upright in activity, ready to accompany Him into the joy and divine palace of His glory, where there is the ceaseless sound of those that keep festival, and the unspeakable delight of those that behold the ineffable beauty of Thy countenance. For Thou art the true Light that enlightenest and sanctifiest all, and all creation doth hymn Thee unto ages of ages. Amen.

Prayer 6, likewise by St. Basil

We bless Thee, O Most High God and Lord of mercy, Who ever doest with us things both great and inscrutable, both glorious and awesome, of which there is no measure; who grantest to us sleep for rest from our infirmities, and relaxation from the labours of our much toiling flesh. We thank Thee that thou hast not destroyed us with our iniquities, but hast shown Thy loving-kindness to man as usual, and while we were lying in despair upon our beds, Thou hast raised us up that we might glorify Thy dominion. Wherefore, we implore Thy boundless goodness: Enlighten the eyes of our understanding and raise up our mind from the heavy sleep of indolence; open our mouth and fill it with Thy praise, that we may be able steadily to hymn and confess Thee, Who art God glorified in all and by all, the unoriginate Father, with Thine Only-begotten Son, and Thine All-holy and good and life-creating Spirit, now and ever, and unto the ages of ages. Amen.

Prayer 7, to the Most Holy Theotokos
I sing of thy grace, O sovereign Lady, and I pray thee to grace my mind. Teach me to step aright in the way of Christ's commandments. Strengthen me to keep awake in song, and drive away the sleep of despondency. O Bride of God, by thy prayers release me, bound with the bonds of sin. Guard me by night and by day, and deliver me from foes that defeat me. O bearer of God the Life-giver, enliven me who am deadened by passions. O bearer of the unwaning Light, enlighten my blinded soul. O marvelous palace of the Master, make me to be a house of the Divine Spirit. O bearer of the Healer, heal the perennial passions of my soul. Guide me to the path of repentance, for I am tossed in the storm of life. Deliver me from eternal fire, and from evil worms, and from Tartarus. Let me not be exposed to the rejoicing of demons, guilty as I am of many sins. Renew me, grown old from senseless sins, O most immaculate one. Present me untouched by all torments, and pray for me to the Master of all. Vouchsafe me to find the joys of heaven with all the saints. O most holy Virgin, hearken unto the voice of thine unprofitable servant. Grant me torrents of

tears, O most pure one, to cleanse my soul from impurity. I offer the groans of my heart to thee unceasingly; strive for me, O Sovereign Lady. Accept my service of supplication and offer it to compassionate God. O thou who art above the angels, raise me above this world's confusion. O Light-bearing heavenly tabernacle, direct the grace of the Spirit in me. I raise my hands and lips in thy praise, defiled as they are by impurity, O all-immaculate one. Deliver me from soul-corrupting evils, and fervently intercede with Christ, to Whom is due honour and worship, now and ever, and unto the ages of ages. Amen.

Prayer 8, to our Lord Jesus Christ
O my plenteously-merciful and all-merciful God, Lord Jesus Christ through Thy great love Thou didst come down and become incarnate so that Thou mightest save all. And again, O Saviour, save me by Thy grace, I pray Thee. For if Thou shouldst save me for my works, this would not be grace or a gift, but rather a duty; yea, Thou Who art great in compassion and ineffable in mercy. For he that believeth in Me, Thou hast said, O my Christ, shall live and never see death. If, then, faith in Thee saveth the desperate, behold, I believe, save me, for Thou art my God and Creator. Let faith instead of works be imputed to me, O my God, for Thou wilt find no works which could justify me. But may my faith suffice instead of all works, may it answer for, may it acquit me, may it make me a partaker of Thine eternal glory. And let Satan not seize me and boast, O Word, that he hath torn me from Thy hand and fold. But whether I desire it or not, save me, O

Christ my Saviour, forestall me quickly, quickly, for I perish. Thou art my God from my mother's womb. Vouchsafe me, O Lord, to love Thee now as fervently as I once loved sin itself, and also to work for Thee without idleness, diligently, as I worked before for deceptive Satan. But supremely shall I work for Thee, my Lord and God, Jesus Christ, all the days of my life, now and ever, and unto the ages of ages. Amen.

Prayer 9, to the Holy Guardian Angel
O holy angel that standeth by my wretched soul and my passionate life, forsake not me a sinner, nor shrink from me because of mine intemperance. Give no place for the cunning demon to master me through the violence of my mortal body, strengthen my poor and feeble hand, and guide me in the way of salvation. Yea, O holy angel of God, guardian and protector of my wretched soul and body, forgive me all wherein I have offended thee all the days of my life; and if I have sinned during the past night, protect me during the present day, and guard me from every temptation of the enemy, that I may not anger God by any sin. And pray to the Lord for me, that He may establish me in His fear, and show me, His servant, to be worthy of His goodness. Amen.

Prayer 10, to the Most Holy Theotokos
O my most holy Lady Theotokos, through thy holy and all-powerful prayers banish from me, thy lowly and wretched servant,

despondency, forgetfulness, folly, carelessness, and all filthy, evil, and blasphemous thoughts from my wretched heart and my darkened mind. Quench the flame of my passions also, for I am poor and wretched, and deliver me from many and cruel memories and deeds, and free me from all their evil effects. For blessed art thou by all generations, and glorified is thy most honorable name unto the ages of ages. Amen.

Prayerful Invocation of the Saint Who's Name we bear.

Pray unto God for me O holy God-pleaser [*Name*], for I fervently flee unto thee, the speedy helper and intercessor for my soul.

Song of the Most Holy Theotokos: *Tone 4*

O Theotokos and Virgin, rejoice, Mary, full of grace, the Lord is with thee; blessed art thou among women, and blessed is the Fruit of thy womb, for thou hast borne the Saviour of our souls.

Troparion to the Cross *Tone 1*

Save, O Lord, Thy people, and bless Thine inheritance; grant Thou victory to Orthodox Christians over enemies; and by the power of Thy Cross do Thou preserve Thy commonwealth.

Then offer a brief prayer for the health and salvation of thy spiritual father, thy parents, relatives, those in authority, benefactors, others known to thee, the ailing, or those passing through sorrows, as follows:

For the Living

Remember, O Lord Jesus Christ our God, Thy mercies and compassions which are from the ages, for the sake of which Thou didst become man and didst will to endure crucifixion and death for the salvation of those that rightly believe in Thee; and having risen from the dead didst ascend into the heavens and sittest at the right hand of God the Father, and regardest the humble entreaties of those that call upon Thee with all their heart; incline Thine ear, and hearken unto the humble supplication of me, Thine unprofitable servant, as an odor of spiritual fragrance, which I offer unto Thee for all Thy people. And first, remember Thy Holy, Catholic, and Apostolic Church, which Thou hast provided through Thy precious Blood, and establish, and strengthen, and expand, increase, pacify, and keep Her unconquerable by the gates of hades; calm the dissensions of the churches, quench the raging of the nations, and quickly destroy and uproot the rising of heresy, and bring them to naught by the power of Thy Holy Spirit.
Bow.
Save, O Lord, and have mercy on this land and her Orthodox people both in the homeland and in the Diaspora.
Bow.
Save, O Lord, and have mercy on the holy Eastern Orthodox patriarchs, most reverend metropolitans, Orthodox archbishops and bishops, and all the priestly and monastic order, and all who serve in the

Church, whom Thou hast appointed to shepherd Thy rational flock, and through their prayers have mercy and save me a sinner.
Bow.
Save, O Lord, and have mercy on my spiritual father [*Name*], and through his holy prayers forgive my sins.
Bow.
Save, O Lord, and have mercy on my parents, [*Names,*] my brothers and sisters, and my kindred according to the flesh, and all the neighbours of my family and friends, and grant them Thine earthly and spiritual good things.
Bow.
Save, O Lord, and have mercy on the aged and the young, the poor and the orphans and widows, and those in sickness and sorrow, misfortune and tribulation, those in difficult circumstances and in captivity, in prisons and dungeons, and especially those of Thy servants that are persecuted for Thy sake and the Orthodox Faith by godless peoples, by apostates, and by heretics; and remember them, visit, strengthen, comfort, and by Thy power quickly grant them relief, freedom, and deliverance.
Bow.
Save, O Lord, and have mercy on them that hate and wrong me, and make temptation for me, and let them not perish because of me, a sinner.
Bow.
Illumine with the light of awareness the apostates from the Orthodox Faith, and those blinded by pernicious heresies, and number them with Thy Holy, Apostolic, Catholic Church.
Bow.

For the Departed
Remember, O Lord, those that have departed this life, Orthodox kings and queens, princes and princesses, most holy patriarchs, most reverend metropolitans, Orthodox archbishops and bishops, those in priestly and clerical orders of the Church, and those that have served Thee in the monastic order, and grant them rest with the saints in Thine eternal tabernacles.
Bow.
Remember, O Lord, the souls of Thy departed servants, my parents, [*Names,*] and all my kindred according to the flesh; and forgive them all transgressions, voluntary and involuntary, granting them the kingdom and a portion of Thine eternal good things, and the delight of Thine endless and blessed life.
Bow.
Remember, O Lord, also all our fathers and brethren, and sisters, and those that lie here, and all Orthodox Christians that departed in the hope of resurrection and life eternal, and settle them with Thy saints, where the light of Thy countenance shall visit them, and have mercy on us, for Thou art good and the Lover of mankind.
Bow.
Grant, O Lord, remission of sins to all our fathers, brethren, and sisters that have departed before us in the faith and hope of resurrection, and make their memory to be eternal.
Bow.

Hymn to the Most Holy Theotokos *Tone 8*
It is truly meet to bless thee, the Theotokos, ever-blessed and most blameless and Mother

of our God. More honorable than the Cherubim, and beyond compare more glorious than the Seraphim, who without corruption gavest birth to God the Word, the very Theotokos, thee do we magnify.

Glory to the Father, and to the Son, and to the Holy Spirit, both now and ever, and unto the ages of ages. Amen.

Lord, have mercy. *Thrice.*

The Prayer of St. Ephraim the Syrian
This prayer is read in all the Holy Great Lent, except on Saturdays and Sundays.

O Lord and Master of my life, a spirit of idleness, despondency, ambition, and idle talking give me not.
Prostration.

But rather a spirit of chastity, humble-mindedness, patience, and love bestow upon me Thy servant.
Prostration.

Yea, O Lord King, grant me to see my failings and not condemn my brother; for blessed art Thou unto the ages of ages. Amen.
Prostration.

O God, cleanse me a sinner. *12 times, with a reverence each time, and then the entire prayer:*

O Lord and Master of my life, a spirit of idleness, despondency, ambition, and idle talking give me

not. But rather a spirit of chastity, humble-mindedness, patience, and love bestow upon me Thy servant. Yea, O Lord King, grant me to see my failings and not condemn my brother; for blessed art Thou unto the ages of ages. Amen.
Prostration.

O Lord Jesus Christ, Son of God, for the sake of the prayers of Thy most pure Mother, our holy and God-bearing fathers and all the saints, have mercy on us. Amen.

God be gracious to us, and shine thy countenance upon us and have mercy on us.

This is the day which the Lord has made; let us rejoice and be glad in it.

Evening Prayers

*[If for some legitimate reason you are not able to recite the full prayer rule, you may say the prayers in **bold type** omitting the others]*

+In the Name of the Father, and of the Son, and of the Holy Spirit. Amen.

O Lord Jesus Christ, Son of God, for the sake of the prayers of Thy most pure Mother, of our holy and God-bearing fathers and all the saints, have mercy on us. Amen.

Glory to Thee, our God, glory to Thee.

Between Pascha and Pentecost we omit "O Heavenly King" and say the following : **Christ is risen from the dead, trampling down death by death, and upon those in the tombs, bestowing life. Thrice.**

O Heavenly King Tone 6
O Heavenly King, Comforter, Spirit of Truth, Who art everywhere present and fillest all things, Treasury of good things and Giver of Life, come and abide in us, and cleanse us of all impurity, and save our souls, O Good One.

Trisagion Tone 6
Holy God, Holy Mighty, Holy Immortal, have mercy on us. *Thrice.*

Glory to the Father, and to the Son, and to the Holy Spirit, both now and ever, and unto the ages of ages. Amen.

O Most Holy Trinity, have mercy on us. O Lord, blot out our sins; O Master, pardon our iniquities; O Holy One, visit and heal our infirmities, for Thy name's sake.

Lord, have mercy. *Thrice.*

Glory to the Father, and to the Son and to the Holy Spirit, both now and ever, and unto the ages of ages. Amen.

Our Father, Who art in the heavens, hallowed be Thy Name. Thy Kingdom come. Thy will be done, on earth as it is in heaven. Give us this day our daily bread. And forgive us our debts as we forgive our debtors. And lead us not into temptation, but deliver us from the evil one.

Troparia Tone 6
Have mercy on us, O Lord, have mercy on us; for at a loss for any defense, this prayer do we sinners offer unto Thee as Master: have mercy on us.

Glory to the Father, and to the Son, and to the Holy Spirit.

Lord, have mercy on us; for we have hoped in Thee, be not angry with us greatly, neither remember our iniquities; but look upon us now as Thou art compassionate, and deliver us from our enemies, for Thou art our God, and we, Thy people; all are the works of Thy

hands, and we call upon Thy name.

Both now and ever, and unto the ages of ages. Amen.

The door of compassion open unto us, O blessed Theotokos, for, hoping in thee, let us not perish; through thee may we be delivered from adversities, for thou art the salvation of the Christian race.

Lord, have mercy. *Twelve times.*

(or during Holy Great Lent the prayer of our holy father Ephraim the Syrian)

The Prayer of St. Ephraim the Syrian
This prayer is read in all the Holy Great Lent, except on Saturdays and Sundays.

O Lord and Master of my life, a spirit of idleness, despondency, ambition, and idle talking give me not.
Prostration.

But rather a spirit of chastity, humble-mindedness, patience, and love bestow upon me Thy servant.
Prostration.

Yea, O Lord King, grant me to see my failings and not condemn my brother; for blessed art Thou unto the ages of ages. Amen.
Prostration.
O God, cleanse me a sinner. *12 times, with a reverence each time, and then the entire prayer:*

O Lord and Master of my life, a spirit of idleness, despondency, ambition, and idle talking give me not. But rather a spirit of chastity, humble-mindedness, patience, and love bestow upon me Thy servant. Yea, O Lord King, grant me to see my failings and not condemn my brother; for blessed art Thou unto the ages of ages. Amen.
Prostration.

Prayer 1, of Macarius the Great
O Eternal God and King of all creation, Who hast granted me to reach this hour, forgive the sins I have committed this day in deed, word, and thought; and cleanse, O Lord, my humble soul of all impurity of flesh and spirit, and grant me, O Lord, to pass the sleep of this night in peace; that, rising from my lowly bed, I may please Thy most holy name all the days of my life, and thwart the enemies, fleshly and bodiless, that war against me. And deliver me, O Lord, from vain thoughts and evil desires which defile me. For Thine is the kingdom, and the power, and the glory: of the Father, and of the Son, and of the Holy Spirit, now and ever, and unto the ages of ages. Amen.

Prayer 2, of St. Antiochus
O Ruler of all, Word of the Father, O Jesus Christ, Thou Who are perfect: For the sake of the plenitude of Thy mercy, never depart from me, but always remain in me, Thy servant. O Jesus, Good Shepherd of Thy sheep, deliver me not over to the sedition of the serpent, and leave me not to the will of Satan,

for the seed of corruption is in me. But do Thou, O Lord, worshipful God, holy King, Jesus Christ, guard me as I sleep by the Unwaning Light, Thy Holy Spirit, by Whom Thou didst sanctify Thy disciples. O Lord, grant me, Thine unworthy servant, Thy salvation upon my bed. Enlighten my mind with the light of understanding of Thy Holy Gospel; my soul, with the love of Thy Cross; my heart, with the purity of Thy word; my body, with Thy passionless Passion. Keep my thought in Thy humility, and raise me up at the proper time for Thy glorification. For most glorified art Thou together with Thine unoriginate Father, and the Most Holy Spirit, unto the ages. Amen.

Prayer 3, to the Holy Spirit
O Lord, Heavenly King, Comforter, Spirit of Truth, show compassion and have mercy on me Thy sinful servant, and loose me from mine unworthiness, and forgive all wherein I have sinned against Thee today as a man, and not only as a man, but even worse than a beast, my sins voluntary and involuntary, known and unknown, whether from youth, and from evil suggestion, or whether from brazenness and despondency. If I have sworn by Thy name, or blasphemed it in my thought; or grieved anyone, or have become angry about anything; or have lied, or slept needlessly, or if a beggar hath come to me and I disdained him; or if I have grieved my brother, or have quarreled, or have condemned anyone; or if I have been boastful, or prideful, or angry; if, as I stood at prayer,

my mind hath been distracted by the wiles of this world, or by thoughts of depravity; if I have over-eaten, or have drunk excessively, or laughed frivolously; if I have thought evil, or seen the beauty of another and been wounded thereby in my heart; if I have said improper things, or derided my brother's sin when mine own sins are countless; if I have been neglectful of prayer, or have done some other wrong that I do not remember, for all of this and more than this have I done: have mercy, O Master my Creator, on me Thy downcast and unworthy servant, and loose me, and remit, and forgive me, for Thou art good and the Lover of mankind, so that, lustful, sinful, and wretched as I am, I may lie down and sleep and rest in peace. And I shall worship, and hymn, and glorify Thy most honourable name, together with the Father and His Only-begotten Son, now and ever, and unto the ages of ages. Amen.

Prayer 4, of St. Macarius the Great

What shall I offer Thee, or what shall I give Thee, O greatly-gifted, immortal King, O compassionate Lord Who lovest mankind? For though I have been slothful in pleasing Thee, and have done nothing good, Thou hast led me to the close of this day that is past, establishing the conversion and salvation of my soul. Be merciful to me a sinner, bereft of every good deed, raise up my fallen soul which hath become defiled by countless sins, and take away from me every evil thought of this visible life. Forgive my sins, O Only Sinless One, in which I have sinned against Thee this day, known or unknown, in word, and deed, and thought, and in all my senses. Do Thou Thyself protect and guard me from every opposing circumstance, by Thy Divine authority and power and inexpressible love for mankind. Blot out, O God, blot out the multitude of my sins. Be pleased, O Lord, to deliver me from the net of the evil one, and save my passionate soul, and overshadow me with the light of Thy countenance when Thou shalt come in glory; and cause me, uncondemned now, to sleep a dreamless sleep, and keep Thy servant untroubled by thoughts, and drive away from me all satanic deeds; and enlighten for me the eyes of my heart with understanding, lest I sleep unto death. And send me an angel of peace, a guardian and guide of my soul and body, that he may deliver me from mine enemies; that, rising from my bed, I may offer Thee prayers of thanksgiving. Yea, O Lord, hearken unto me, Thy sinful and wretched servant, in confession and conscience; grant me, when I arise, to be instructed by Thy sayings; and through Thine angels cause demonic despondency to be driven far from me: that I may bless Thy holy name, and glorify and extol the most pure Theotokos Mary, whom Thou hast given to us sinners as a protectress, and accept her who prayeth for us. For I know that she exemplifieth Thy love for mankind and prayeth for us without ceasing. Through her protection, and the sign of the precious Cross, and for the sake of all Thy saints, preserve my wretched soul, O Jesus Christ our God: for holy art Thou, and most glorious forever. Amen.

Prayer 5
O Lord our God, as Thou art good and the Lover of mankind, forgive me wherein I have sinned today in word, deed and thought. Grant me peaceful and undisturbed sleep; send Thy guardian angel to protect and keep me from all evil. For Thou art the Guardian of our souls and bodies, and unto Thee do we send up glory: to the Father, and to the Son, and to the Holy Spirit, now and ever, and unto the ages of ages. Amen.

Prayer 6
O Lord our God, in Whom we believe and Whose name we invoke above every name, grant us, as we go to sleep, relaxation of soul and body, and keep us from all dreams and dark pleasures; stop the onslaught of the passions and quench the burnings that arise in the flesh. Grant us to live chastely in deed and word, that we may obtain a virtuous life, and not fall away from Thy promised blessings; for blessed art Thou forever. Amen.

Prayer 7, of St. John Chrysostom, according to the number of hours of day and night.
O Lord, deprive me not of Thy heavenly good things. O Lord, deliver me from eternal torments. O Lord, if I have sinned in mind or thought, in word or deed, forgive me. O Lord, deliver me from all ignorance, forgetfulness, faint-heartedness, and stony insensibility. O Lord, deliver me from every temptation. O Lord, enlighten my heart which evil desire hath darkened. O Lord, as a man I have sinned, but do Thou, as the compassionate God,

have mercy on me, seeing the infirmity of my soul. O Lord, send Thy grace to my aid, that I may glorify Thy holy name. O Lord Jesus Christ, inscribe me Thy servant in the Book of Life, and grant me a good end. O Lord my God, even though I have done nothing good in Thy sight, yet grant me by Thy grace to make a good beginning. O Lord, sprinkle into my heart the dew of Thy grace. O Lord of heaven and earth, remember me Thy sinful servant, shameful and unclean, in Thy kingdom. Amen.

O Lord, accept me in penitence. O Lord, forsake me not. O Lord, lead me not into temptation. O Lord, grant me good thoughts. O Lord, grant me tears, remembrance of death, and compunction. O Lord, grant me the thought of confessing my sins. O Lord, grant me humility, chastity, and obedience. O Lord, grant me patience, courage, and meekness. O Lord, implant in me the root of good, Thy fear in my heart. O Lord, vouchsafe me to love Thee with all my soul and mind, and in all things to do Thy will. O Lord, protect me from evil men, demons, and passions, and from every other unseemly thing. O Lord, I know that Thou doest as; Thou wilt: Thy will be done also in me a sinner; for blessed art Thou unto the ages. Amen.

Prayer 8, to our Lord Jesus Christ

O Lord Jesus Christ, Son of God, for the sake of Thy most honourable Mother, and Thy bodiless angels, Thy Prophet and Forerunner and Baptist, the God-inspired apostles, the radiant and victorious martyrs, the holy and God-bearing fathers, and through the intercessions of all the saints, deliver me from the besetting presence of the demons. Yea, my Lord and Creator, Who desirest not the death of a sinner, but rather that he be converted and live, grant conversion also to me, wretched and unworthy; rescue me from the mouth of the pernicious serpent, who is yawning to devour me and take me down to hades alive. Yea, my Lord, my Comfort, Who for my miserable sake wast clothed in corruptible flesh, draw me out of misery, and grant comfort to my miserable soul. Implant in my heart to fulfill Thy commandments, and to forsake evil deeds, and to obtain Thy blessings; for in Thee, O Lord, have I hoped, save me.

Prayer 9, to the Most Holy Theotokos
O good Mother of the Good King, most pure and blessed Theotokos Mary, do thou pour out the mercy of thy Son and our God upon my passionate soul, and by thine intercessions guide me unto good works, that I may pass the remaining time of my life without blemish, and attain paradise through thee, O Virgin Theotokos, who alone art pure and blessed.

Prayer 10, to the Holy Guardian Angel
O Angel of Christ, my holy guardian and protector of my soul and body, forgive me all wherein I have sinned this day, and deliver me from all opposing evil of mine enemy, lest I anger my God by any sin. Pray for me, a sinful and unworthy servant, that thou mayest show me forth worthy of the kindness and mercy of the All-holy Trinity,

and of the Mother of my Lord Jesus Christ, and all the saints. Amen.

Kontakion to the Theotokos Tone 8
To thee, the Champion Leader, we thy servants dedicate a feast of victory and of thanksgiving as ones rescued out of sufferings, O Theotokos; but as thou art one with might which is invincible, from all dangers that can be do thou deliver us, that we may cry to thee: Rejoice, thou Bride Unwedded.

Most glorious, Ever-Virgin, Mother of Christ God, present our prayer to thy Son and our God, that through thee He may save our souls.

All my hope I place in thee, O Mother of God: keep me under thy protection.

O Virgin Theotokos, disdain not me a sinner, needing thy help and thy protection, and have mercy on me, for my soul hath hoped in thee.

My hope is the Father, my refuge is the Son, my protection is the Holy Spirit: O Holy Trinity, glory to Thee.

Hymn to the Most Holy Theotokos Tone 8
It is truly meet to bless thee, the Theotokos, ever-blessed and most blameless and Mother of our God. More honorable than the Cherubim, and beyond compare more glorious than the Seraphim, who without corruption gavest birth to God the Word, the very Theotokos, thee do we magnify.

Glory to the Father, and to the Son, and to the Holy Spirit, both now and ever, and unto the ages of ages. Amen.

Lord, have mercy. *Thrice.*

O Lord Jesus Christ, Son of God, for the sake of the prayers of Thy most pure Mother, our holy and God-bearing fathers and all the saints, have mercy on us. Amen.

Prayer of Saint John Damascene, which is to be said while pointing at thy bed:
O Master, Lover of mankind, is this bed to be my coffin, or wilt Thou enlighten my wretched soul with another day? Behold, the coffin lieth before me; behold, death confronteth me. I fear, O Lord, Thy judgment and the endless torments, yet I cease not to do evil. My Lord God, I continually anger Thee, and Thy most pure Mother, and all the Heavenly Hosts, and my Holy Guardian Angel. I know, O Lord, that I am unworthy of Thy love for mankind, but am worthy of every condemnation and torment. But, O Lord, whether I will it or not, save me. For to save a righteous man is no great thing, and to have mercy on the pure is nothing wonderful, for they are worthy of Thy mercy. But on me a sinner, show the wonder of Thy mercy; in this reveal Thy love for mankind, lest my wickedness prevail over Thine ineffable goodness and merciful kindness; and order my life as Thou wilt.

Prayer for the departed
With the saints, give rest, O Christ, to the

souls of thy servants where there is no pain, no sorrow, no sighing, but life everlasting.

And when about to lie down in bed, say this:

Enlighten mine eyes, O Christ God, lest at any time I sleep unto death, lest at any time mine enemy say: I have prevailed against him.

Glory to the Father, and to the Son, and to the Holy Spirit.

Be my soul's helper, O God, for I pass through the midst of many snares; deliver me out of them and save me, O Good One, for Thou art the Lover of mankind.

Both now and ever, and unto the ages of ages. Amen.

The most glorious Mother of God, more holy than the holy angels, let us hymn unceasingly with our hearts and mouths, confessing her to be the Theotokos, for truly she gaveth birth to God incarnate for us, and prayeth unceasingly for our souls.

Then, in lieu of asking forgiveness of others;

Remit, pardon, forgive, O God, our offenses, both voluntary and involuntary, in deed and word, in knowledge and ignorance, by day or by night, in mind and thought; forgive us all things, for Thou art good and the Lover of mankind.

Prayer
O Lord, Lover of mankind, forgive them that hate and wrong us. Do good to them that do good. Grant our brethren and kindred their saving petitions and life eternal; visit the infirm and grant them healing. Guide those at sea. Journey with them that travel. Help Orthodox Christians to struggle. To them that serve and are kind to us grant remission of sins. On them that have charged us, the unworthy, to pray for them, have mercy according to Thy great mercy. Remember, O Lord, our fathers and brethren de-parted before us, and grant them rest where the light of Thy countenance shall visit them. Remember, O Lord, our brethren in captivity, and deliver them from every misfortune. Remember, O Lord, those that bear fruit and do good works in Thy holy churches, and grant them their saving petitions and life eternal. Remember also, O Lord, us Thy lowly and sinful and unworthy servants, and enlighten our minds with the light of Thy knowledge, and guide us in the way of Thy commandments; through the intercessions of our most pure Lady, the Theotokos and Ever-Virgin Mary, and of all Thy saints, for blessed art Thou unto the ages of ages. Amen.

Daily Confession of Sins

I confess to Thee, my Lord God and Creator, in one Holy Trinity glorified and worshipped, to the Father, Son, and Holy Spirit, all my sins which I have committed in all the days of my life, and at every hour, at the present time and in the past, day and night, by deed, word, thought, gluttony, drunkenness, secret eating, idle talking, despondency, indolence, contradiction, disobedience, slandering, condemning, negligence, self-love, acquisitiveness, extortion, lying, dishonesty, mercenariness, jealousy, envy, anger, remembrance of wrongs, hatred, bribery; and by all my senses: sight, hearing, smell, taste, touch; and by the rest of my sins, of the soul together with the bodily, through which I have angered Thee, my God and Creator, and dealt unjustly with my neighbour. Sorrowing for these, I stand guilty before Thee, my God, but I have the will to repent. Only help me, O Lord my God, with tears I humbly entreat Thee. Forgive my past sins through Thy compassion, and absolve from all these which I have said in Thy presence, for Thou art good and the Lover of mankind.

Then kiss thy Cross, and make the sign of the Cross from the head to the foot of the bed, and likewise from side to side, while saying:

The Prayer to the Precious Cross

Let God arise and let His enemies be scattered, and let them that hate Him flee from before His face. As smoke vanisheth, so let them vanish; as wax melteth before the fire, so let the demons perish from the presence of them that love God and who sign

themselves with the sign of the Cross and say in gladness: Rejoice, most precious and life-giving Cross of the Lord, for Thou drivest away the demons by the power of our Lord Jesus Christ Who was crucified on thee, Who went down to hades and trampled on the power of the devil, and gave us thee, His precious Cross, for the driving away of every adversary. O most precious and life-giving Cross of the Lord, help me together with the holy Lady Virgin Theotokos, and with all the saints, unto the ages. Amen.

Compass me about, O Lord, with the power of Thy precious and life-giving Cross and preserve me from every evil.

At the time of sleep, say:
Into Thy hands, O Lord Jesus Christ my God, I commit my spirit. Do Thou bless me, do Thou have mercy on me, and grant me life eternal. Amen.

The Order of Preparation for Communion

In the name of the Father, and of the Son, and of the Holy Spirit. Amen.

Through the prayers of our holy fathers, O Lord Jesus Christ our God, have mercy on us. Amen.

Glory to Thee, our God, glory to Thee.

Between Pascha and Pentecost we omit "O Heavenly King" and say the following : **Christ is risen from the dead, trampling down death by death, and upon those in the tombs, bestowing life.** *Thrice.*

O Heavenly King, Comforter, Spirit of Truth, Who art everywhere present and fillest all things, Treasury of good things and Giver of Life, come and dwell in us, and cleanse us of all impurity, and save our souls, O Good One.

Trisagion
Holy God, Holy Mighty, Holy Immortal, have mercy on us. *Thrice.*

Glory to the Father, and to the Son, and to the Holy Spirit, both now and ever, and unto the ages of ages. Amen.

O Most Holy Trinity, have mercy on us. O Lord, blot out our sins; O Master, pardon our iniquities; O Holy One, visit and heal our infirmities, for Thy name's sake.

Lord, have mercy. *Thrice.*

Glory to the Father, and to the Son, and to the Holy Spirit, both now and ever, and unto the ages of ages. Amen.

Our Father, Who art in the heavens, hallowed be Thy Name. Thy kingdom come. Thy will be done, on earth as it is in heaven. Give us this day our daily bread. And forgive us our debts as we forgive our debtors. And lead us not into temptation, but deliver us from the evil one.

Lord, have mercy. *Twelve times.*

Glory to the Father, and to the Son, and to the Holy Spirit, both now and ever, and unto the ages of ages. Amen.

O Come, let us worship God, our King.
Bow.
O Come, let us worship and fall down before Christ, our King and God.
Bow.
O Come, let us worship and fall down before Christ himself, our King and God.
Bow.

Psalm 22
The Lord is my Shepherd, and I shall not want. In a place of green pasture, there hath He made me to dwell; beside the water of rest hath He nurtured me.

He hath converted my soul, He hath led me on the paths of righteousness for His name's sake. For though I should walk in the midst of the shadow of death, I will fear no evil, for Thou art with me; Thy rod and Thy staff, they have comforted me. Thou hast prepared a table for me in the presence of them that afflict me. Thou hast anointed my head with oil, and Thy cup which filleth me, how excellent it is! And Thy mercy shall pursue me all the days of my life, and I will dwell in the house of the Lord unto length of days.

Psalm 23
The earth is the Lord's, and the fullness thereof, the world, and all that dwell therein. He hath founded it upon the seas, and upon the rivers hath He prepared it. Who shall ascend into the mountain of the Lord? Or who shall stand in His holy place? He that is innocent in hands and pure in heart, who hath not received his soul in vain, and hath not sworn deceitfully to his neighbour. Such a one shall receive a blessing from the Lord, and mercy from God his Saviour. This is the generation of them that seek the Lord, of them that seek the face of the God of Jacob. Lift up your gates, O ye princes; and be ye lifted up, ye everlasting gates, and the King of Glory shall enter in. Who is this King of Glory? The Lord strong and mighty, the Lord, mighty in war. Lift up your gates, O ye princes; and be ye lifted up, ye everlasting gates, and the King of Glory shall enter in. Who is this King of Glory? The Lord of hosts, He is the King of Glory.

Psalm 115

I believed wherefore I spake; I was humbled exceedingly. As for me, I said in mine ecstasy; every man is a liar. What shall I render unto the Lord for all that He hath rendered unto me? I will take the cup of salvation, and I will call upon the name of the Lord. My vows unto the Lord will I pay in the presence of all His people. Precious in the sight of the Lord is the death of His saints. O Lord, I am Thy servant; I am Thy servant and the son of Thy handmaid. Thou hast broken my bonds asunder. I will sacrifice a sacrifice of praise unto Thee, and I will call upon the name of the Lord. My vows unto the Lord will I pay in the presence of all His people, in the courts of the house of the Lord, in the midst of thee, O Jerusalem.

Glory to the Father, and to the Son, and to the Holy Spirit, both now and ever, and unto the ages of ages. Amen.

Alleluia, alleluia, alleluia. Glory to Thee, O God. *Thrice.*

Lord, have mercy. *Thrice.*

Troparia, *Tone 8*

Disregard my transgressions, O Lord Who was born of a Virgin, and purify my heart, and make it a temple for Thy spotless Body and Blood. Let me not be rejected from Thy presence, O Thou Who hast great mercy without measure.

Glory to the Father, and to the Son, and to the Holy Spirit.

How can I who am unworthy dare to come to the Communion of Thy Holy Things? For if I should dare to approach Thee with those that are worthy, my garment betrayeth me, for it is not a festal robe, and I shall cause the condemnation of my greatly-sinful soul. Cleanse, O Lord, the pollution from my soul, and save me, as Thou art the Lover of mankind.

Both now and ever, and unto the ages of ages. Amen.

Greatly multiplied, O Theotokos, are my sins; unto Thee have I fled, O pure one, imploring salvation. Do thou visit mine enfeebled soul, and pray to thy Son and our God that He grant me forgiveness for the evil I have done, O thou only blessed one.

During Holy and Great Lent say this:

When the glorious disciples were enlightened at the washing of the feet, then Judas the ungodly one was stricken and darkened with the love of silver. And unto the lawless judges did he deliver Thee, the righteous Judge. Behold, O lover of money, him that for the sake thereof did hang himself; flee from that insatiable soul that dared such things against the Master. O Thou Who art good unto all, Lord, glory be to Thee.

Psalm 50
Have mercy on me, O God, according to Thy great mercy; and according to the multitude of Thy compassions blot out my transgression. Wash me thoroughly from mine iniquity, and cleanse me from my sin. For I

know mine iniquity, and my sin is ever before me. Against Thee only have I sinned and done this evil before Thee, that Thou mightest be justified in Thy words, and prevail when Thou art judged. For behold, I was conceived in iniquities, and in sins did my mother bear me. For behold, Thou hast loved truth; the hidden and secret things of Thy wisdom hast Thou made manifest unto me. Thou shalt sprinkle me with hyssop, and I shall be made clean; Thou shalt wash me, and I shall be made whiter than snow. Thou shalt make me to hear joy and gladness; the bones that be humbled, they shall rejoice. Turn Thy face away from my sins, and blot out all mine iniquities. Create in me a clean heart, O God, and renew a right spirit within me. Cast me not away from Thy presence, and take not Thy Holy Spirit from me. Restore unto me the joy of Thy salvation and with Thy governing Spirit establish me. I shall teach transgressors Thy ways, and the ungodly shall turn back unto Thee. Deliver me from blood-guiltiness, O God, Thou God of my salvation; my tongue shall rejoice in Thy righteousness. O Lord, Thou shalt open my lips, and my mouth shall declare Thy praise. For if Thou hadst desired sacrifice, I had given it; with whole-burnt offerings Thou shalt not be pleased. A sacrifice unto God is a broken spirit; a heart that is broken and humbled God will not despise. Do good, O Lord, in Thy good pleasure unto Sion, and let the walls of Jerusalem be builded. Then shalt Thou be pleased with a sacrifice of righteousness, with oblation and wholeburnt offerings. Then shall they offer bullocks upon Thine altar.

And Immediately.

Canon of Preparation for Holy Communion,
Second Tone

Ode I
Irmos: Come, O you people, let us sing a hymn to Christ our God, Who divided the sea, and guided the people whom He brought out of the bondage of Egypt; for He is glorified.

Refrain: Create in me a clean heart, O God, and renew a right spirit within me.

Troparia: May Thy holy Body be for me the Bread of life eternal, O Compassionate Lord, and may Thy precious Blood also the healing for my many forms of illness.

Refrain: Cast me not away from Thy presence, and take not Thy Holy Spirit from me.

Defiled by unseemly deeds, I the wretched one am unworthy, O Christ, of the communion of Thy most pure Body and divine Blood, which do Thou vouchsafe me.

Glory to the Father, and to the Son, and to the Holy

Spirit, both now and ever, and unto the ages of ages. Amen.

Theotokion: **O blessed Bride of God, O good soil that grew the Corn untilled and saving to the world, vouchsafe me to be saved by eating it.**

Ode III
Irmos: **By establishing me on the rock of faith, Thou hast enlarged my mouth over mine enemies, for my spirit rejoices when I sing: There is none holy as our God, and none righteous beside Thee, O Lord.**

Create in me a clean heart, O God, and renew a right spirit within me.

May Thy most pure Body and divine Blood be unto me for remission of sins, for communion with the Holy Spirit and unto life eternal, O Lover of mankind, and to estrangement of passions and sorrows.

Glory to the Father, and to the Son, and to the Holy Spirit, both now and ever, and unto the ages of ages. Amen.

Theotokion: **O thou most holy table of the Bread of Life that for mercy's sake came down from on high, giving new life to the world, vouchsafe even me, the unworthy, to eat it with fear, and live.**

Ode IV

Irmos: From a Virgin didst Thou come, not as an ambassador, nor as an angel, but the very Lord Himself incarnate, and didst save me, the whole man. Wherefore, I cry to Thee: Glory to Thy power, O Lord.

Create in me a clean heart, O God, and renew a right spirit within me.

Troparia: O Thou Who wast incarnate for our sake, O Most-merciful One, Thou didst will to be slain as a sheep for the sins of mankind. Wherefore I entreat Thee to blot out my sins also.

Cast me not away from Thy presence, and take not Thy Holy Spirit from me.

Heal the wounds of my soul, O Lord, and sanctify all of me, and vouchsafe, O Master, that I the wretched one may partake of Thy divine Mystical Supper.

Glory to the Father, and to the Son, and to the Holy Spirit, both now and ever, and unto the ages of ages. Amen.

Theotokion: Propitiate for me also, Him that came from thy womb, O Lady, and keep me, thy servant, undefiled and blameless, so that by obtaining the spiritual pearl I may be sanctified.

Ode V
Irmos: O Lord, Giver of light and Creator of the ages, guide us in the light of Thy commandments, for we know none other God beside Thee.

Create in me a clean heart, O God, and renew a right spirit within me.

Troparia: As Thou didst foretell, O Christ, let it be to Thy wicked servant, and in me abide as Thou didst promise; for behold, I eat Thy divine Body and drink Thy Blood.

Cast me not away from Thy presence, and take not Thy Holy Spirit from me.

O Word of God and God, may the live coal of Thy Body be unto the enlightenment of me who am in darkness, and Thy Blood unto the cleansing of my defiled soul.

Glory to the Father, and to the Son, and to the Holy Spirit, both now and ever, and unto the ages of ages. Amen.

Theotokion: O Mary, Mother of God, precious tabernacle of fragrance, through thy prayers make me a chosen vessel, that I may partake of the Sacrament of thy Son.

Ode VI
Irmos: Whirled about in the abyss of sin, I appeal to the unfathomable abyss of Thy

compassion: From corruption raise me up, O God.

Create in me a clean heart, O God, and renew a right spirit within me.

Troparia: **O Saviour, sanctify my mind, soul, heart and body, and vouchsafe me uncondemned, O Master, to approach the fearful Mysteries.**

Cast me not away from Thy presence, and take not Thy Holy Spirit from me.

Grant that I may be rid of passions, and the assistance of Thy grace, and strengthening of life by the communion of Thy holy Mysteries, O Christ.

Glory to the Father, and to the Son, and to the Holy Spirit, both now and ever, and unto the ages of ages. Amen.

Theotokion: **O Holy Word of God and God, sanctify all of me as I now come to Thy divine Mysteries, through the prayers of Thy holy Mother.**

Lord, have mercy. *Thrice.*

Glory to the Father, and to the Son, and to the Holy Spirit, both now and ever, and unto the ages of ages. Amen.

Kontakion, Tone 2:
Count me not unworthy, O Christ, to receive

now the Bread which is Thy Body, and Thy divine Blood, and to partake, O Master, of Thy most pure and dread Mysteries, wretched though I be. Let these not be for me unto judgment, but unto life immortal and everlasting.

Ode VII
Irmos: The wise children did not serve the golden image, but went themselves into the flame and reviled the pagan gods. They cried in the midst of the flame, and the angel bedewed them: Already the prayer of your lips was heard.

Create in me a clean heart, O God, and renew a right spirit within me.

Troparia: May the communion of Thine immortal Mysteries, the source of blessings, O Christ, be to me now light, and life, and dispassion and for progress and increase in the most divine virtues, O only Good One, that I may glorify Thee.

Cast me not away from Thy presence, and take not Thy Holy Spirit from me.

That I may be delivered from passions, enemies, need, and every sorrow, I now draw nigh with trembling, love and reverence, O Lover of mankind, to Thine immortal and divine Mysteries. Vouch-safe me to hymn Thee: Blessed art Thou, O Lord God of our fathers.

Glory to the Father, and to the Son, and to the Holy Spirit, both now and ever, and unto the ages of ages. Amen.

Theotokion: O thou who art full of grace, who beyond understanding gavest birth to Christ the Saviour, I thy servant, the impure, now entreat thee, the pure: Cleanse me, who am now about to approach the most pure Mysteries, from all defilement of flesh and spirit.

Ode VIII
Irmos: God Who descended into the fiery furnace unto the Hebrew children and changed the flame into dew, praise Him as Lord O ye works, and supremely exalt Him unto all the ages.

Create in me a clean heart, O God, and renew a right spirit within me.

Troparia: Of Thy heavenly, dread and holy Mysteries, O Christ, and of Thy divine Mystical Supper, vouchsafe now even me, the despairing one, to partake O God my Savior.

Cast me not away from Thy presence, and take not Thy Holy Spirit from me.

Fleeing for refuge to Thy loving-kindness, O Good One, with fear I cry unto Thee: Abide in me, O Saviour, and I, as Thou hast said in Thee. For behold, presuming on Thy mercy, I eat Thy Body and drink Thy Blood.

Glory to the Father, and to the Son, and to the Holy Spirit, both now and ever, and unto the ages of ages. Amen.

Triadicon: I tremble at taking fire, lest I be consumed as wax and grass. O fearful Mystery! O loving-kindness of God! How is it that I, being but clay, partake of the divine Body and Blood, and am made incorruptible?

Ode IX
Irmos: The Son of the unoriginate Father, God and Lord, hath appeared unto us incarnate of a Virgin, to enlighten those in darkness, and to gather the dispersed. Wherefore the all-hymned Theotokos do we magnify.

Create in me a clean heart, O God, and renew a right spirit within me.

Troparia: Christ It is, O taste and see! The Lord for our sake made like unto us of old, once offered Himself as an offering to His Father, and is ever slain, sanctifying them that partake.

Cast me not away from Thy presence, and take not Thy Holy Spirit from me.

May I be sanctified in soul and body, O Master; may I be enlightened, may I be saved, may I become Thy dwelling through the communion of Thy holy Mysteries, having Thee with the Father and the Spirit living in me, O Benefactor, plenteous in mercy.

Glory to the Father, and to the Son, and to the Holy Spirit.

May Thy Body and Thy most precious Blood, O my Saviour, be unto me as fire and light, consuming the substance of sin and burning the thorns of passions, and enlightening all of me to worship Thy Divinity.

Both now and ever, and unto the ages of ages. Amen.

Theotokion: God took flesh of thy pure blood; wherefore, all generations do hymn thee, O Lady, and throngs of heavenly minds glorify thee, for through thee they have clearly seen Him Who ruleth all things endued with human nature.

Hymn to the Most Holy Theotokos, Tone 8
It is truly meet to bless thee, the Theotokos, ever-blessed and most blameless and Mother of our God. More honourable than the Cherubim, and beyond compare more glorious than the Seraphim, who without corruption gavest birth to God the Word, the very Theotokos, thee do we magnify.

Trisagion
Holy God, Holy Mighty, Holy Immortal, have mercy on us. *Thrice.*

Glory to the Father, and to the Son, and to the Holy Spirit, both now and ever, and unto the ages of ages. Amen.

O Most Holy Trinity, have mercy on us. O Lord, blot out our sins; O Master, pardon our iniquities; O Holy One, visit and heal our infirmities, for Thy name's sake.

Lord, have mercy. *Thrice.*

Glory to the Father, and to the Son, and to the Holy Spirit, both now and ever, and unto the ages of ages. Amen.

Our Father, Who art in the heavens, hallowed be Thy Name. Thy kingdom come. Thy will be done, on earth as it is in heaven. Give us this day our daily bread. And forgive us our debts as we forgive our debtors. And lead us not into temptation, but deliver us from the evil one.

On Sunday, the : of the Resurrection of the tone (see pg. 79, Appendix A). For a feast of the Lord, the troparion of the feast (see pg. 83, Appendix B). If not, the following:

Troparia, Tone 6:
Have mercy on us, O Lord, have mercy on us; for at a loss for any defense, this prayer do we sinners offer unto Thee as Master: Have mercy on us.

Glory to the Father, and to the Son, and to the Holy Spirit.
Lord, have mercy on us, for we have hoped in Thee, be not angry with us greatly, neither remember our iniquities; but look upon us now as Thou art

compassionate, and deliver us from our enemies; for Thou art our God, and we, Thy people; all are the works of Thy hands, and we call upon Thy name.

Both now and ever, and unto the ages of ages. Amen.

The door of compassion open unto us, O blessed Theotokos, for, hoping in thee, let us not perish; through thee may we be delivered from adversities, for thou art the salvation of the Christian race.

Then: **Lord, have mercy.** *Forty times.*

Bows or prostrations, as many as desired.

And thereafter these lines:
If thou desirest, O man, to eat the Body of the Master.
Approach with fear, lest thou be burnt; for It is fire.
And when thou drinkest the Divine Blood unto communion.
First be reconciled to them that have grieved thee.
Then dare to eat the Mystical Food.

In the morning upon arising:

+ In the Name of the Father, and of the Son, and of the Holy Spirit. Amen.

Glory to Thee, our God, glory to Thee.

Between Pascha and Pentecost we omit "O Heavenly King" and say the following : **Christ is risen from the dead, trampling down death by death, and upon those in the tombs, bestowing life.** *Thrice.*

O Heavenly King Tone 6
O Heavenly King, Comforter, Spirit of Truth, Who art everywhere present and fillest all things, Treasury of good things and Giver of Life, come and dwell in us, and cleanse us of all impurity, and save our souls, O Good One.

Trisagion
Holy God, Holy Mighty, Holy Immortal, have mercy on us. *Thrice.*

Lord, have mercy. *Thrice.*

Glory to the Father, and to the Son and to the Holy Spirit, both now and ever, and unto the ages of ages. Amen.

Our Father, Who art in the heavens, hallowed be Thy Name. Thy Kingdom come. Thy will be done, on earth as it is in heaven. Give us this day our daily bread. And forgive us our debts as we forgive our debtors. And lead us not into temptation, but deliver us from the evil one.

Lord, have mercy. *Twelve times.*

Glory to the Father, and to the Son and to the Holy Spirit, both now and ever, and unto the ages of ages. Amen.

O Come, let us worship God, our King.
Bow.

O Come, let us worship and fall down before Christ, our King and God.
Bow.
O Come, let us worship and fall down before Christ himself, our King and God.
Bow.

A Prayer of Basil the Great, 1:
O Master Lord Jesus Christ our God, Source of life and immortality, Creator of all things visible and invisible, the co-eternal and co-unoriginate Son of the unoriginate Father, Who, out of Thy great goodness, didst in the latter days clothe Thyself in flesh, and wast crucified, and buried for us ungrateful and evil-disposed ones, and hast renewed with Thine Own Blood our nature corrupted by sin: Do Thou Thyself, O Immortal King, accept the repentance of me a sinner, and incline Thine ear to me, and hearken unto my words. For I have sinned against heaven and before Thee, and I am not worthy to look upon the height of Thy glory; for I have angered Thy goodness by transgressing Thy commandments and not obeying Thine injunctions. But Thou, O Lord, Who art not vengeful, but long-suffering and plenteous in mercy, hast not given me over to be destroyed with my sins, but always Thou awaitest my complete conversion. For Thou hast said, O Lover of mankind, through Thy prophet: For I desire not the death of the sinner, but that he should return and live. For Thou desirest not, O Master, to destroy

the work of thy hands, neither shalt Thou be pleased with the destruction of men, but desirest that all be saved and come to a knowledge of the truth. Wherefore, even I, although unworthy of heaven and earth, and of this temporal life, having submitted my whole self to sin, and made myself a slave of pleasure, and having defaced Thine image, yet being Thy work and creation, wretched though I be, I despair not of my salvation, and dare to approach Thine immeasurable loving-kindness. Accept, then, even me, O Lord, Lover of mankind, as Thou didst accept the sinful woman, the thief, the publican, and the prodigal; and take away the heavy burden of my sins, Thou that takest away the sin of the world, and healest the infirmities of mankind, Who callest the weary and heavy-laden unto Thyself and givest them rest, Who camest not to call the righteous, but sinners to repentance. And do Thou cleanse me from all defilement of flesh and spirit, and teach me to achieve holiness in fear of Thee; that with the pure testimony of my conscience, receiving a portion of Thy Holy Things, I may be united unto Thy Holy Body and Blood, and have Thee living and abiding in me with the Father and Thy Holy Spirit. Yea, O Lord Jesus Christ my God, let not the communion of Thine immaculate and life-giving Mysteries be unto me for judgment, neither unto infirmity of soul and body because of my partaking of them unworthily; but grant me until my last breath to receive without condemnation the portion of Thy Holy Things, unto communion with the Holy Spirit, as a provision for life eternal, for an acceptable defense at Thy dread judgment seat; so that I also, with all Thine elect, may become a partaker of Thine incorruptible blessings, which Thou hast prepared for them that love Thee, O Lord, in whom Thou art glorified unto the ages. Amen.

A Prayer of St. John Chrysostom, 2:
O Lord My God, I know that I am not worthy nor sufficient that Thou shouldest enter beneath the roof of the temple of my soul, for all is empty and fallen, and Thou hast not in me a place worthy to lay Thy head; but as from on high Thou didst humble Thyself for our sake, do Thou now also lower Thyself to my lowliness; and as Thou didst consent to lie in a cave and in a manger of dumb beasts, so consent also to lie in the manger of mine irrational soul and to enter into my defiled body. And as Thou didst not refuse to enter and to dine with sinners in the house of Simon the Leper, so deign also to enter into the house of my lowly soul, leprous and sinful. And as Thou didst not reject the harlot and sinner like me, when she came and touched Thee, so be compassionate also with me a sinner, as I approach and touch Thee. And as Thou didst feel no loathing for the defiled and unclean lips of her that kissed Thee, do Thou also not loathe my

defiled lips nor mine abominable and impure mouth, and my polluted and unclean tongue. But let the fiery coal of Thy most Holy Body and Thy precious Blood be unto me for sanctification and enlightenment and health for my lowly soul and body, unto the lightening of the burden of my many sins, for preservation from every act of the devil, for the expulsion and prohibition of mine evil and wicked habits, unto the mortification of the passions, unto the keeping of Thy commandments, unto the application of Thy divine grace, unto the acquiring of Thy kingdom. For not with disdain do I approach Thee, O Christ God, but as one trusting in Thine ineffable goodness, and that I may not by much abstaining from Thy communion become the prey of the spiritual wolf. Wherefore do I entreat Thee, for Thou art the only Holy One, O Master: Sanctify my soul and body, my mind and heart, my belly and inward parts, and renew me entirely; and implant Thy fear in my members, and make Thy sanctification inalienable from me, and be unto me a helper and de-fender, guiding my life in peace, vouchsafing me also to stand at Thy right hand with Thy saints, through the intercessions and supplications of Thy most pure Mother, of Thine immaterial ministers and immaculate hosts, and of all the saints who from the ages have been pleasing unto Thee. Amen.

Prayer of Symeon Metaphrastes, 3:
O only pure and sinless Lord, Who, through the ineffable compassion of Thy love for mankind, didst take on all of our substance from the pure and virgin blood of her that bare Thee supernaturally through the descent of the Divine Spirit and the good will of the everlasting Father; O Christ Jesus, Wisdom of God, and Peace, and Power, Thou Who through the assumption of our nature didst take upon Thyself Thy life-giving and saving Passion: the Cross, the nails, the spear, and death: Mortify the soul-corrupting passions of my body. Thou Who by Thy burial didst lead captive the kingdom of hades, bury with good thoughts mine evil schemes, and destroy the spirits of evil. Thou Who by Thy life-bearing Resurrection on the third day didst raise up our fallen forefather, raise me up who have slipped down into sin, setting before me the ways of repentance. Thou Who by Thy most glorious Ascension didst deify the flesh that Thou hadst taken, and didst honour it with a seat at the right hand of the Father, vouchsafe me through partaking of Thy holy Mysteries to obtain a place at Thy right hand among them that are saved. O Thou Who by the descent of Thy Spirit, the Comforter, didst make Thy holy disciples worthy vessels, show me also to be a receptacle of His coming. Thou Who art to come again to judge the world in righteousness, deign to let me also meet Thee on the clouds, my Judge and Creator, with all

Thy saints; that I may endlessly glorify and praise Thee, with Thine unoriginate Father, and Thy Most-Holy and good and life-creating Spirit, now and ever, and unto the ages of ages. Amen.

Prayer of the Divine Damascene, 4:
O Master Lord Jesus Christ our God, Who alone hast authority to remit the sins of men: Do Thou, as the Good One and Lover of mankind, overlook all mine offences, whether committed with knowledge or in ignorance. And vouchsafe me to partake without condemnation of Thy Divine, glorious, immaculate, and life-giving Mysteries; not as a burden, nor for punishment, nor for an increase of sins, but unto purification and sanctification, and as a pledge of the life and kingdom to come, as a bulwark and help, and for the destruction of enemies, and for the blotting out of my many transgressions. For Thou art a God of mercy, and compassion, and love for mankind, and unto Thee do we send up glory, with the Father, and the Holy Spirit, both now and ever, and unto the ages of ages. Amen.

Prayer of St. Basil the Great, 5:
I know, O Lord, that I partake unworthily of Thine immaculate Body and Thy precious Blood, and that I am guilty, and eat and drink damnation to myself, not discerning the Body and Blood of Thee, my Christ and God; but taking courage from Thy

compassion I approach Thee Who hast said: He that eateth My Flesh, and drinketh My Blood, abideth in Me and I in him. Show compassion, therefore, O Lord, and do not accuse me, a sinner, but deal with me according to Thy mercy; and let these Holy Things be for me unto healing, and purification, and enlightenment, and preservation, and salvation, and unto sanctification of soul and body; unto the driving away of every phantasy, and evil practice, and activity of the devil working mentally in my members; unto confidence and love toward Thee, unto correction of life, unto steadfastness, unto an increase of virtue and perfection, unto fulfillment of the commandments, unto communion with the Holy Spirit, as a provision for life eternal, as an acceptable defense at Thy dread tribunal, not unto judgment or condemnation.

Prayer of St. Symeon the New Theologian, 6: From sullied lips, from an abominable heart, from a tongue impure, from a soul defiled, accept my supplication, O my Christ, and disdain me not, neither my words, nor my ways, nor my shamelessness. Grant me to say boldly that which I desire, O my Christ. Or rather, teach me what I ought to do and say. I have sinned more than the sinful woman who, having learned where Thou wast lodging, bought myrrh, and came daringly to anoint Thy feet, my God, my Master, and my Christ. As Thou didst not reject her when she drew near from her heart, neither, O Word, be Thou filled with loathing for me, but grant me Thy feet to clasp and kiss, and with floods of tears, as with most precious myrrh, dare to anoint them. Wash me with my tears, and purify me with them, O Word; remit also my transgressions, and grant me pardon. Thou knowest the multitude of mine evils, Thou knowest also my sores, and Thou seest my wounds; but also Thou knowest my faith and Thou beholdest my good intentions, and Thou hearest my sighs. Nothing is hidden from Thee, my God, my Creator, my Redeemer, neither a tear-drop, nor a part of a drop. My deeds not yet done Thine eyes have seen, and in Thy book even things not yet accomplished are written by Thee. See my lowliness, see my toil, how great it is, and all my sins take from me, O God of all; that with a pure heart, a trembling mind, and a contrite soul I may partake of Thy spotless and most holy Mysteries, by which all that eat and drink in purity of heart are quickened and deified. For Thou, O my Master, hast said: Everyone that eateth My Flesh and drinketh My Blood abideth in Me, and I in him. True is every word of my Master and God; for whosoever partaketh of the divine and deifying grace is no more alone, but with Thee, my Christ, the three-sunned Light that enlighteneth the world. And that I may not remain alone without Thee, the Life-giver, my Breath, my Life, my

Rejoicing, the Salvation of the world, therefore have I drawn nigh unto Thee, as Thou seest, with tears, and with a contrite soul. O Ransom of mine offences, I ask Thee to receive me, and that I may partake without condemnation of Thy life giving and perfect Mysteries, that Thou mayest remain, as Thou hast said, with me, a thrice-wretched one, lest the deceiver, finding me without Thy grace, craftily seize me, and having beguiled me, draw me away from Thy deifying words. Wherefore, I fall down before Thee, and fervently cry unto Thee: As Thou did receive the prodigal, and the sinful woman who drew near, so receive me, the prodigal and profligate, O Compassionate One. With contrite soul I now come to Thee. I know, O Saviour, that none other hath sinned against Thee as have I, nor hath wrought the deeds that I have done. But this again I know, that neither the magnitude of mine offences nor the multitude of my sins surpasseth the abundant long-suffering of my God and His exceeding love for mankind; but with sympathetic mercy Thou dost purify and illumine them that fervently repent, and makest them partakers of the light, sharers of Thy divinity without stint. And, strange to angels and to the minds of men, Thou conversest with them oft times, as with Thy true friends. These things make me bold, these things give me wings, O Christ. And taking courage from the wealth of Thy benefactions to us, rejoicing and trembling at once, I partake of Fire, I that am grass. And, strange wonder! I am bedewed without being consumed, as the bush of old burned without being consumed. Now with thankful mind, and grateful heart, with thankfulness in my members, my soul and body, I worship and magnify and glorify Thee, my God, for blessed art Thou, both now and unto the ages.

Prayer of St. John Chrysostom, 7:
O God, loose, remit, and pardon me my transgressions wherein I have sinned against Thee, whether by word, deed, or thought, voluntarily or involuntarily, consciously or unconsciously; forgive me all, for Thou art good and the Lover of man-kind. And through the intercessions of Thy most pure Mother, Thy noetic ministers and holy hosts, and all the saints who from the ages have been pleasing unto Thee, deign to allow me without condemnation to receive Thy holy and immaculate Body and precious Blood, unto the healing of soul and body, and unto the purification of mine evil thoughts. For Thine is the kingdom, and the power, and the glory, with the Father and the Holy Spirit, now and ever, and unto the ages of ages. Amen.

Prayer of the same, 8:
I am not sufficient, O Master and Lord, that Thou shouldest enter under the roof of my soul; but as Thou dost will as the Lover of

mankind to dwell in me, I dare to approach Thee. Thou commandest: I shall open the doors which Thou alone didst create, that Thou mayest enter with Thy love for mankind, as is Thy nature, that Thou mayest enter and enlighten my darkened thought. I believe that Thou wilt do this, for Thou didst not drive away the sinful woman when she came unto Thee with tears, neither didst Thou reject the publican who repented, nor didst Thou spurn the thief who acknowledged Thy kingdom, nor didst Thou leave the repentant persecutor to himself; but all of them that came unto Thee in repentance Thou didst number among Thy friends, O Thou Who alone art blessed, always, now and unto endless ages. Amen.

Prayer of the same, 9:
O Lord Jesus Christ my God, loose, remit, cleanse, and forgive me, Thy sinful and unprofitable, and unworthy servant, my transgressions and offences and fallings into sin, which I have committed against Thee from my youth until the present day and hour, whether consciously or unconsciously, whether by words or deeds, or in thought or imagination, in habit, and in all my senses. And through the intercessions of her that seedlessly gave Thee birth, the most pure and Ever-Virgin Mary, Thy Mother, the only hope that maketh not ashamed, and my mediation and salvation, vouchsafe me without condemnation to partake of Thine

immaculate, immortal, life-giving and awesome Mysteries, unto the remission of sins and for life eternal, unto sanctification and enlightenment, strength, healing, and health of both soul and body, and unto the consumption and complete destruction of mine evil reasonings and intentions and prejudices and nocturnal phantasies of dark and evil spirits; for Thine is the kingdom, and the power, and the glory, and the honour and the worship, with the Father and Thy Holy Spirit, now and ever, and unto the ages of ages. Amen.

Another Prayer of St. John Damascene, 10:
I stand before the doors of Thy temple, yet I do not put away evil thoughts. But do Thou, O Christ God, Who didst justify the publican, and didst have mercy on the woman of Canaan, and didst open the doors of paradise to the thief, open unto me the abyss of Thy love for mankind, and receive me as I come and touch Thee, as Thou didst receive the sinful woman and the woman with an issue of blood. For the one received healing easily by touching the hem of Thy garment, while the other, by clasping Thy most pure feet, carried away absolution of sins. And I, a wretch, daring to receive Thy whole Body, let me not be consumed by fire; but receive me, as Thou didst receive them, and enlighten my spiritual senses, burning up my sinful errors; through the intercessions of her that seedlessly gave Thee birth, and of the

heavenly hosts, for blessed art Thou unto the ages of ages. Amen.

Another Prayer of Chrysostom:
I believe, O Lord and I confess that Thou art truly the Christ, the Son of the living God, Who came into the world to save sinners, of whom I am chief. Moreover, I believe that this is truly Thy most pure Body, and this is truly Thine Own precious Blood; wherefore, I pray Thee: Have mercy on me and forgive me my transgressions, voluntary and involuntary, whether in word or deed, in knowledge or in ignorance. And vouchsafe me to partake without condemnation of Thy most pure Mysteries, unto the remission of sins and life everlasting. Amen.

When coming to partake, say to thyself these lines of Metaphrastes.

Behold, I approach the Divine Communion O Creator, let me not be burnt by communicating. For Thou art Fire, consuming the unworthy But, rather, purify me of all impurity.

Then again say:

Of Thy Mystical Supper, O Son of God, receive me today as a communicant; for I will not speak of the Mystery to Thine enemies; neither like Judas will I give Thee a kiss, but like the thief will I confess Thee: Remember me, O Lord, in Thy kingdom.

Furthermore, these lines:

Be awe-stricken, O mortal, beholding the deifying Blood;
For It is a fire that consumeth the unworthy.
The Divine Body both deifieth and nourisheth me.
It deifieth the spirit, and wondrously nourisheth the mind.

Then the Troparia:

Thou hast sweetened me with Thy love, O Christ, and by Thy Divine zeal hast Thou changed me. But do Thou consume my sins with immaterial fire, and vouchsafe me to be filled with delight in Thee; that, leaping for joy, O Good One, I may magnify Thy two comings. Into the brilliant company of Thy saints how shall I the unworthy enter? For if I dare to enter into the bridechamber, my garment betrayeth me, for it is not a wedding garment and I shall be bound and cast out by the angels. Cleanse, O Lord, my soul of pollution, and save me, as Thou art the Lover of mankind.

Then the Prayer:

O Master, Lover of mankind, O Lord Jesus Christ my God, let not these Holy Things be unto me for judgment, through my being unworthy, but unto the purification and sanctification of soul and body, and as a pledge of the life and kingdom to come. For it

is good for me to cleave unto God, to put my hope of salvation in the Lord.

And again:

Of Thy Mystical Supper, O Son of God, receive me today as a communicant; for I will not speak of the Mystery to Thine enemies; neither, like Judas, will I give Thee a kiss; but like the thief will I confess Thee: Remember me, O Lord, in Thy kingdom.

A Preparation for Confession

by

St. John of Kronstadt

I, a sinful soul, confess to our Lord God and Savior Jesus Christ, all of my evil acts which I have done, said or thought from baptism even unto this present day.

I have not kept the vows of my baptism, but have made myself unwanted before the face of God.

I have sinned before the Lord by lack of faith and by doubts concerning the Orthodox Faith and the Holy Church; by ungratefulness for all of God's great and unceasing gifts; His long-suffering and His providence for me, a sinner; by lack of love for the Lord, as well as fear, through not fulfilling the Holy Commandments of God and the canons and rules of the Church.

I have not preserved a love for God and for my neighbor, nor have I made enough efforts, because of laziness and lack of care, to learn the Commandments of God and the precepts of the Holy Fathers.

I have sinned: by not praying in the morning and in the evening and in the course of the day; by not attending the services or by coming to Church only half-heartedly, lazily and carelessly; by conversing during the services, by not paying attention, letting my mind wander and by departure from the Church before the dismissal and blessing.

I have sinned by judging members of the clergy.

I have sinned by not respecting the Feasts, breaking the Fasts, and by immoderation in food and drink.

I have sinned by self-importance, disobedience, willfulness, self-righteousness, and the seeking of approval and praise.

I have sinned by unbelief, lack of faith, doubts, despair, despondency, abusive thoughts, blasphemy and swearing.

I have sinned by pride, a high opinion of my self, narcissism, vanity, conceit, envy, love of praise, love of honors, and by putting on airs.

I have sinned: by judging, malicious gossip, anger, remembering of offenses done to me, hatred and returning evil for evil; by slander, reproaches, lies, slyness, deception and hypocrisy; by prejudices, arguments, stubbornness, and an unwillingness to give way to my neighbor; by gloating, spitefulness, taunting, insults and mocking; by gossip, by speaking too much and by empty speech.

I have sinned by unnecessary and excessive laughter, by reviling and dwelling upon my previous sins, by arrogant behavior, insolence and lack of respect.

I have sinned by not keeping my physical and spiritual passions in check, by my enjoyment of impure thoughts, licentiousness and unchastity in thoughts, words and deeds.

I have sinned by lack of endurance towards my illnesses and sorrows, a devotion to the comforts of life and by being too attached to my parents, children, relatives and friends.

I have sinned by hardening my heart, having a weak will and by not forcing myself to do good.

I have sinned by miserliness, a love of money, the acquisition of unnecessary things and immoderate attachment to things.

I have sinned by self-justification, a disregard for the admonitions of my conscience and failing to confess my sins through negligence or false pride.

I have sinned many times by my Confession: belittling, justifying and keeping silent about sins.

I have sinned against the Most-holy and Life-creating Mysteries of the Body and Blood of our Lord by coming to Holy Communion without humility or the fear of God.

I have sinned in deed, word and thought, knowingly and unknowingly, willingly and unwillingly, thoughtfully and thoughtlessly, and it is impossible to enumerate all of my sins because of their multitude. But I truly repent of these and all others not mentioned by me because of my forgetfulness and I ask that they be forgiven through the abundance of the Mercy of God.

Appendix A

Troparion of the Resurrection:

Tone 1
When the stone had been sealed by the Jews, and the soldiers were guarding Thine immaculate Body, Thou didst arise on the third day, O Saviour, granting life unto the world. Wherefore, the Hosts of the heavens cried out to Thee, O Life-giver: Glory to Thy Resurrection, O Christ. Glory to Thy Kingdom. Glory to Thy dispensation, O only Lover of mankind.

Tone 2
When Thou didst descend unto death, O Life Immortal, then didst Thou slay hades with the lightning of Thy Divinity. And when Thou didst also raise the dead out of the nethermost depths, all the Hosts of the heavens cried out: O Life-giver; Christ or God, glory be to Thee.

Tone 3
Let the heavens be glad; let earthly things rejoice; for the Lord hath wrought might with His arm. He hath trampled down death by death; the firstborn of the dead hath He become. From the belly of hades hath He delivered us and hath granted to the world great mercy.

Tone 4
Having learned the joyful proclamation of the Resurrection from the angel, and having cast off the ancestral condemnation, the women disciples of the Lord spake to the apostles exultantly: Death is

despoiled and Christ God is risen, granting to the world great mercy.

Tone 5
Let us, O faithful, praise and worship the Word Who is co-unoriginate with the Father and the Spirit, and Who was born of the Virgin for our salvation; for He was pleased to ascend the Cross in the flesh and to endure death, and to raise the dead by His glorious Resurrection.

Tone 6
Angelic Hosts were above Thy tomb, and they that guarded Thee became as dead. And Mary stood by the grave seeking Thine immaculate Body. Thou didst despoil hades and wast not tempted by it. Thou didst meet the Virgin and didst grant us life. O Thou Who didst rise from the dead, O Lord, glory be to Thee.

Tone 7
Thou didst destroy death by Thy Cross; Thou didst open Paradise to the thief. Thou didst change the lamentation of the Myrrh-bearers, and Thou didst command Thine Apostles to proclaim that Thou didst arise, O Christ God, and grantest to the world great mercy.

Tone 8
From on high didst Thou descend, O Compassionate One; to burial of three days hast Thou submitted that Thou mightest free us from our passions. O our Life and Resurrection, O Lord, glory be to Thee.

Appendix B

Feasts of the Lord
Troparion of the feast:

The Exaltation of the Cross
(14 September)
Tone 1

O Lord, save Thy people and bless Thine inheritance, granting Orthodox Christians victory over their enemies, and guarding Thy commonwealth with Thy Cross.

The Nativity of Christ our Lord
(25 December)
Tone 4

Thy Nativity, O Christ our God, has shone upon the world with the light of knowledge: for thereby they who adored the stars through a star were taught to worship Thee, the Sun of Righteousness, and to know Thee the Dayspring from on high. O Lord, glory to Thee.

Theophany
(6 January)
Tone 1

When Thou, O Lord, wast baptized in the Jordan, the worship of the Trinity was made manifest. For the voice of the Father bore witness unto Thee, calling Thee the beloved Son, and the Spirit in the form of a dove confirmed His word as sure and steadfast. O Christ of God who has appeared and enlightened the world, glory to Thee.

Palm Sunday
(One week before Pascha)
Tone 1

Giving us before Thy Passion an assurance of the general resurrection, Thou hast raised Lazarus from the dead, O Christ our God. Therefore, like the children, we also carry tokens of victory, and cry to Thee, the Conqueror of death: Hosanna in the highest; blessed is He that comes in the Name of the Lord. (*Twice*)

The Ascension of Our Lord
(40 days after Pascha)
Tone 4

Thou hast ascended in glory, O Christ or God, having gladdened Thy disciples with the promise of the Holy Spirit; and they were assured by the blessing that Thou art the Son of God, the Redeemer of the world.

Pentecost
(Trinity Sunday: 50 days after Pascha)
Tone 8

Blessed art Thou, O Christ our God, Who hast shown forth the fishermen as supremely wise, by sending down upon them the Holy Spirit, and through them didst draw the world into Thy net. O Lover of mankind, glory be to Thee.

The Transfiguration of Our Lord
(6 August)
Tone 7

Thou wast transfigured upon the mountain, O Christ our God, showing Thy glory to Thy disciples as far as they were able to bear it. At the intercessions of the Theotokos, make Thine everlasting light shine forth also upon us sinners. O Giver of light, glory to Thee.

The Living
List here those living you want to pray for.

The Living
List here those living you want to pray for.

The Living
List here those living you want to pray for.

The Living
List here those living you want to pray for.

The Living
List here those living you want to pray for.

The Living
List here those living you want to pray for.

The Departed
List those departed this life that you want to pray for.

The Departed

List those departed this life that you want to pray for.

The Departed
List those departed this life that you want to pray for.

The Departed
List those departed this life that you want to pray for.

The Departed
List those departed this life that you want to pray for.

The Departed

List those departed this life that you want to pray for.

Printed in Great Britain
by Amazon.co.uk, Ltd.,
Marston Gate.